SURRENDER
TO
GRAVITY

KIRA NICOLE JOHNSON

Surrender To Gravity

Copyright © 2024 by Kira Nicole Johnson.

MILTON & HUGO L.L.C.
4407 Park Ave., Suite 5
Union City, NJ 07087, USA

Website: *www. miltonandhugo.com*
Hotline: *1- 888-778-0033*
Email: *info@miltonandhugo.com*

Ordering Information:
Quantity sales. Special discounts are granted to corporations, associations, and other organizations. For more information on these discounts, please reach out to the publisher using the contact information provided above.

Library of Congress Control Number: 2024922445
ISBN-13:   979-8-89285-352-1   [Paperback Edition]
                  979-8-89285-353-8   [Digital Edition]

Rev. date: 10/25/2024

CONTENTS

This book is for the women I've once loved, those who have left me with sweet memories, impactful lessons, and lasting scars.

PART 1

the ways i loved

off paper

i haven't learned to love you
off paper
quite yet
but when i tap away
at my keyboard
in a way only i do,
the tapping sound
becomes a song,
a symphony to be precise
one directed by my dazzling love for you
as i fight for a sliver of your attention
and hope my written art
sent to capture your heart
receives a standing ovation
or even just a glance in my direction
as i play together verses formed of
pompous adjectives and the sweetest nouns
to follow a chorus of metaphors

i pine after you endlessly
alone in an apartment
much too large for just one person
sprawled across an unvacuumed floor
the remains of crumpled letters to you
littering the itchy carpet
all in attempt to display my love
because in the end,
i'm terribly afraid
that you walked away
from what we almost had
not because you love her instead
but because you don't understand
the way i love you

i haven't learned to love you
off paper
quite yet
to open my mouth
which is known to stumble over sentences
and form my lips around spoken desire
but just know that it is
because i love you so much
that these words on paper
are just much too heavy
and much too loud
to be held by
only the air between us

i haven't learned to love you
off paper
quite yet
so i sit at this keyboard
hands still in defeat
wrestling with the thought
of mustering up
just enough courage
to give courage to the
i love you
to let each word lift up
off these pages
and fly out of my throat
declaring my love
off paper

for now it remains a thing
of the future
one i'll write down in
the cluttered lines of my agenda
right next to
start that business
apply to that school
publish that book
and all the other
things i want desperately
yet fear with shaky breaths
threatening to consume me whole

but maybe, just maybe
one day i'll part my lips
in a wild display of courage
and i'll learn to love you
off paper/

recipe for disaster

1/2 sapphic compatibility
1 warm femininity
1 denied sexuality

pour until intensified

4 liquor-soaked lips
100 honey-coated lies
1 closet hidden lust

the loyal lesbian

you can wrap chains around my ankles
and put ropes on my wrists
you can torture me day and night
and aim your words like daggers
but just know that
my love will be unmoving

you can throw me in a dungeon
and bolt the doors for eternity
you can let the darkness eat me alive
and leave me to die in the filth of confusion
but just know that
my love will be unstoppable

you can burn my body alive
and set fire to all that i hold dear
you can watch what remains of me
drift upwards in an angry plume of smoke
but just know that
my love will be undying

but if you hold me close to you
and declare your loyalty under the stars
or have a steady shoulder
for me to lean upon
just know that
my love will run from you

ten ways to love someone who'll never love you back

1. bend yourself into a twisted shape
    so she can always lean on you
2. soften your scarred skin
    so you can gently brush away her tears
3. lose nights of sleep and days of peace
    just to write and rewrite and rewrite letters
    perfecting each word until
    your metaphors are almost as perfect as her
4. learn every little fact about her
    as if she is the handbook
    to surviving the first love
5. keep her secrets locked away
    in the farthest reaches of your heart
    and protect them with your life
6. understand that silence is rooted
    in the pain she grew from
7. know that red flags turn green in the dark
8. recognize that some love,
    no matter how pure and precious
    just can't be
9. never utter a word of things
    confessed in the hours of night
10. beware that at any moment
    she could disappear
    like the moon at sunrise

she was much too good for me

she
was filled
with the softest moonlight
the kind that filters through the trees
and guides the hearts of those utterly lost
she embodied gentle power

i
was filled
with powerful flames
the kind that will warm you through the winter
but burn you if you get too close
i embodied chaotic love

hold me till morning

i always held walls
on every side
of my chaos
until you
then i forgot what even
walls were

the physique of an angel

i love you
i love everything about you
your beauty is simply unfathomable
the bouncing curls of your dark hair
tied back to show off the delicacy
of your countenance
one that shines
with compassion and serenity
while your precious smile spreads light
to parts of my heart
that have only ever known darkness
and the way those hips sway
with attitude and vivacity
makes my body tremble
at the thought of being beneath yours
looking up into the pooling depths of your irises
and marvel at the chance to
behold
the physique
of an angel

no harm

i promise i mean no harm
but overpowering is the need
to express the feelings blazing within
the farthest reaches of my heart
but this love is much too
twisted with fragility
and so i will only whisper
my lost mumblings
to this secret-soaked paper

finding love

if there was a room
filled with all the things
i've ever lost
and i could only have
one thing back
i think
i'd run to you
without hesitation
but I say
i think
because what if you
aren't in my room
and instead I am in yours
because you lost me

i stormed you

like rain,
i fell for you
soft at first
powerful at once
steady as always
in sync to my heartbeat
never ceasing to jump each time we spoke
but you...
you turned your face away
and ran for cover far from the rain

so like hail,
i came for you
breaking every rule,
hurling past any warnings,
stopping at nothing,
to reach the warmth of your arms
but you locked the doors
and bolted the windows
to shut me out

then like snow,

i was called beautiful yet wished gone

so i melted away

into the background

of a damaged heart and broken soul

and whispered three words

into the freezing night air

"but we almost..."

to love me

if i lay on the floor of the depths
of the ocean in search of meaning
would you be a ray of light reaching me
even as i lay there unconscious, limp
waiting for someone to breathe life back into me
would you be the one...

if i tried to steal a star from the night sky
in search of guidance
but fell back to earth
would you be a net to catch me
even as the air whipped past my tiny frame
and i slipped through the sky's empty hands
would you be the one...

if i crawled towards a raging fire in search of warmth
but the flames licked my skin
would you kiss my burns
even as i fell into the ashes and coals
praying for healing hands
to carry me to safety
would you be the one...

if i bloomed into a precious rose in search of love
but also grew many thorns along the way
would you cradle me in your tranquility
even as i drew blood from your veins
and pulled tears from your eyes
wishing i was without these imperfections
would you be the one...

these goddamn stars

you told me that it wasn't written
upon the constellations
for our hearts
to be intertwined
yet so many other things
were not written above
but still took place in time
but within my hands
and within your hands
we hold the pen of choice
and in wielding such
we could cause
every limitation
to disappear
every obstacle
to m
     e
      l
        t
and every barrier
to e v a p o r a t e
until nothing stood between
me and my love
if the sun and the moon chase each other endlessly
always stopping to kiss good morning
and wink goodnight
why can't we also

you told me that it wasn't
written upon the constellations
for our hearts to be intertwined
but my beautiful love,
did you forget?
writing is what i do best...

moonlight lips

she speaks sweet light
into my utter darkness
with her moonlight lips
each word spoken
flows with beauty and hope
the sound of her tenderly powerful voice
is like a soothing medicine on open wounds
her verbiage strings together
like the lines of stars above
connecting into constellations of meaning

all that comes from her moonlight lips
her whispers
her shouts
her laughter
her jokes
her secrets

i only wish to know what moonlight tastes like...

humiliated

i told you it was
simply a speech impediment
that made me trip my words
but you and i both know
it was not my tongue
but my pride
that i was choking on

Go Right Ahead

if you're going to break my heart
go right ahead and break it
but promise you'll do it so gently
shatter it but make it fast
hit me so i may fall into a deep slumber
and arise only when i have healed

if you're going to break my heart
go right ahead and break it
but promise to warn me first
smash it but tell me of your intentions before
so that i may ready myself for the impact
and harden my heart for the torment

if you're going to break my heart
go right ahead and break it
but know what comes next
i may lie in tearful defeat for awhile
but then i'll be back up on my feet
ready to taste the sweet flavor of revenge
hurt me sweetheart,
and i'll hurt you ten times worse
if you're going to break my heart
know that it always
heals stronger
so good fucking luck

dangerously lovely

remember that i am a rose
a rose dripping
red from the blood of my enemies
but i am also more
i am a rose
a rose spreading
wide leaves to shelter the weaker flowers
from the harshest weathers

i am made of layers
layers of fragile delicate petals
whose beauty weaves itself
through my intricate simplicities

remember that i am a rose
deep, symbolic and metaphorical
dancing through life
in the shadows yet always noticed

i am a law of nature
within the simple fact that i am a delicate flower
yet i have found ways to protect myself
always remember that i am a rose
but never forget that i come with thorns

umbrella

you'll still feel the wind,
but i'll take the rain
i'll protect you from the roughest of the storm
and you'll lay me to dry
in your glowing warmth

not meant to be

but I wanted you
and you wanted me
even though we were never meant to be
that is the most soulful way
to fall in love

the lover who chases endlessly
and the runner who denies their truth
in a net of secrecy
a tangle of hope
a web of anticipation

let them have their feeble meant to be story
i want our never meant to be legend

beware of her beauty

i always fall back in love
with that vivacious woman
who has the capability
to hurt me beyond comprehension
with all her wild eccentricities
weaved into gleaming effervescence
and i'm always left shot down
whispering to my tired heart
"beware of her beauty"
"beware of loving her"
"beware of saying too much"

dreaming of a woman

the wind blew a dream into me
of something both
intense and invisible
fearful and powerful
protective and comforting
assiduous and loyal
unwavering and unshakable
soft and strong
and one day I'll look you in the eyes
and tell you just how perfect our love would've been

level up, my darling

the girl is higher than
the perspective
but the lover is lower than
the standard
so i float
somewhere in the middle of desire and patience

miracle love

make me believe
in miracles
i want you to give me proof
that the butterflies in my stomach
are just in their cocoons,
but not dead
i want you to give me proof
that all the voices in my head are wrong
screaming in my ear
that you are no different
i *want* you to be different
i *know* you are different
you *have* to be different
so go on
coax down my walls
with firm kindness
gently remove the barbed wire
with resilient care
melt away my love
buried inside a lonely iceberg
and while it will be painful
for us both
maybe even terrifying
for us both
please gather enough courage
to make me believe
in miracles

with you

with
lips stained
from
women never deserving of her
she
kissed me soft

with
a heart wrecked
from
those before my time
she
offered sweet love

with
words guarded
from
memories of betrayal
she
told me her truths

with
arms broken
from
holding up the solar system
we
held each other tight

your backup plan

oh baby, tease me
with no intentions of love
pull me so close
but call me a maybe
sway those curved hips
and flirt your very best
lick your sweet lips
ensnare me with a smirk
and an eyebrow raise
tell me to stay in your arms awhile
but don't think I don't know
what it is you're doing

your sapphic fantasy

leave me the scraps of your attention
and i will feast upon them
make me your play thing
your sapphic fantasy
and i will offer myself to your every desire
my yet unbroken heart
i sacrifice to you, my queen
to be your experimental love
i bare my form in all its innocence
so that you may take what you please
and leave the rest

love soaked in fear

i will swallow your conscience whole
run my tongue along your jagged edges
take a bite out of your aching pain
chew up your screaming doubts

and then spit you out

i will leave you
but not until you recognize
your value and worth
and not before you learn to love
your sweet reflection

sound therapy

i even memorized
the sweet sound
of her laughter

there's the three-syllable laugh
a ha-ha-ha followed by
ohmyyyygoshhhhh
in which all the resolve
fades off of her face
and is replaced with a reason
for me to hope

then there's the giggle
that escapes her lips
and she nods her head softly
with a smile still remaining
on her warm face

but my favorite is
when her waves of laughter
fill the void inside of me
and her body leans forward
as if some part of her soul is trying
to reach into
the spark filled air between us
and freeze the moment
and now i'm laughing with her
and im not sure i even know the joke

baby i'm lost

i stumble forward
through each day
eyes downcast
in a visual definition of defeat
arms feebly outstretched before me
in hopes my hand will brush against yours
and you'll lead me with patience
through these murky mists
as if you're the compass
and i'm the wandering nomad
as if you're the maps
and i'm the reason we're lost
as if you love me
and i love you with all my
lost pieces

best described as indescribable

i've met so many people
in my short number of years
i've met sweet people
with swirls of heaven
in their emerald eyes
and i've met angry people
with slivers of hell
in their artic-blue eyes
i've met stony gray-eyed businessmen
and i've met the softest brown-eyed strippers
i've met children with effervescent bright eyes
and i've met seniors with wise translucent eyes
i've carefully wiped tears from pained eyes
and i've watched grieving eyes crinkle in laughter
i've met many people
and seen countless pairs of eyes
each magnificently unique

but *her* eyes
oh god, *her* eyes
what her eyes do to me
is best described
as indescribable

inside the whites of her eyes
surge the deep chestnut shade of her irises
the same ones that turn to onyx when angered
melting into her pupils
silencing those who speak with ignorance
then soften into sweet umber when at peace
spreading infectious laughter and tenderness
soft lashes line her expressive eyelids
stealing away any hope i ever had
at escaping the spell
those chestnut eyes cast upon me they are simply
best described
as indescribable

what her eyes do to me
is beyond comprehension
her eyes are full of a light
brighter than all of mother teresa's good deeds
pinching at the corners
when a smile spreads across her face
they are the eyes
that remain impossible to forget
imbedded into my brain
pulling me in again and again
and even though i consider myself a rooted woman
those eyes will always drown me in a power
best described
as indescribable

balanced

i live this existence
on a tightrope
crafted from patience
worn so thin,
it's almost translucent…
yet every time
you enter a room
my breath stops
and I could walk
this dangerous
tightrope
forever

where did you come from

are you an angel speaking in tongues
or a demon breathing fiery lies
some days i burn from
the flames of this love
as if you've trapped me in hell
and other days i bask in the glow of your love
as if you're the only heaven there is
i just can't decipher
when i press my lips to yours
if you're the sweetest holy water
or just another poisoned apple

insanity

they called me brave

they called me strong

they called me unstoppable

and they called me fearless

little do they know

curled up inside me

like a hungry poised snake

ready to strike at any moment

lies my fears

my deepest being the inevitability of insanity

i fear the day i could

subtly drift into a blindness to reality

and lose myself piece by piece

soliloquizing in isolation

and tearing at my skin

grabbing my hair in fists

and trying to form my lips around jumbled syllables

this is my fear

my deepest fear

every day it creeps into the back of my brain
like robbers in the quiet
when will it happen?
just how crazy will i go?
is it possible to escape the curse?
every damn day
the hamster wheel of terror
turns endlessly behind this fearless mask

but then

i sat next to you

and you spoke to me

and i felt a wave of peace wash over me
and a hush of quiet settle inside of me
for the first time
i wasn't afraid
of going crazy

somehow

in your presence

all thoughts rooted in fear flee my mind

and all i can focus on is how magnificent you are

the sight of your eyes

block visions of padded rooms

the sound of your voice

overbear the ones i fear i will hear one day

the taste of your lips

become the only medicine i will ever need

when i'm with you

i'm brave

i'm strong

i'm unstoppable

i'm fearless

when i'm with you

my only fear is losing you

not exactly heartless

i'm kind of cruel
but only because
I know what
cruel kindness feels like

it's the little things about you

smiling with only half your face sometimes
as if a full smile is reserved for special occasions only
taking ear to each lyric within a song
staying on the phone till you drift off into sleep
putting your whole heart and soul into each thing you do
hating mustard
making weird little sounds when you're bored
saying pop out loud every single time you pop your gum
looking upward and pursing your lips when angered
only owning three pieces of jewelry
dimples peeking out when you smile
holding my eye contact with intensity that could melt me
wearing the same enchanting fragrance every day
closing your eyes when you kissed me
and then keeping them closed as if either of us opened our eyes
we'd realize it was but a dream held inside an hourglass
holding my fragility so gently in your arms
tracing my spine with your fingertips
like a blind woman feeling the braille word for connection
breaking my heart so viciously yet so softly
you loved me, even if only for a moment
and then you didn't but it's okay

    i'll never forget the little things about you

texture

i had a heart of determined steel
but legs of wet paper
a resolve set into hardened stone
but words softer than smoke

as much as i do

the ocean
in love with the land
reaching to the shore
in an attempt
to save all the pieces
of her broken shells
within her graspless waves

she pulls back
but never to give up
only to attempt again tomorrow
until she saves every last piece
of her broken shells
littered across the sands

day after day
never ceasing
to attempt the impossible
in the name of love
but is that love?

the antagonists

she's the one
that makes a devil
fall in love with her
bringing a being of evil
to its knees
eyes downcast
and filling with tears
horns sawed down
in a commitment to change
tail tucked in fear of
unconditional love

she's the one
that makes a giant
whisper of its secrets
hands shaking
as they attempt to be gentle with her
lightly treading upon
the unfamiliar ground of
acceptance

she's the one
who makes a villain
want to save the world for her
face flooding
with warm emotion
harsh words
softening into laughter
no longer hiding behind masks
of cold intelligence

she's the one
that makes a monster
cease to roar
in her powerful presence
bowing its head in peace
so she may reach out her hand
and soothe the instincts
of an uncontrollable creature

she's the one
that falls for the bad ones
for within them
she sees herself

natural disaster

i was but a heavy rainstorm
of haunting memories
my heart flowed out
in the liquid of my sad eyes
i crashed down to the earth
with intensity and despair
falling
falling
falling
but like a chasm in the earth
you opened yourself to me
letting my rain fall onto
the craggy cliff walls
of your own experiences
i watered the flowers
that grew in the cracks of your insecurities
and you gave me a safe place to crash land

"love"

such a tender word
coated in power and strength
yet still so tender

although slippery on most tongues
it remains frozen in my throat
and rough against my lips

it brings life
it causes death
it heals
it wounds

the four letters
like a rusty knife deep in my chest
imbedded permanently
paralyzing me in pain
yet the only thing keeping me
from bleeding out

the same four letters
like a magical roaring river
healing power washing over me
soothing my burns and blisters
a medicine for my wounds
making me whole again

"love"
so strange a word to speak
uttered like a foreign language
in a land of confusion
if only i knew what this word meant
if only i knew

learning to love again

she engulfed me
in all that i am
and she veiled over
all that i am not
she made love to my faults
and caressed my flaws
kissed my fallen petals
and stroked my thorns
she felt my pain
and thought no less
of my dark
for she also
knew of secrets lurking
in the pitch-black dark

you can't figure me out

when aphrodite breathed life into me
celestial duties were paused
the underworld's commotion halted
and all fell silent

the angels gasped in utter shock
while the demons shook their heads in disbelief
for my sweet halo of diamonds
sat atop a pair
of red poison-tipped horns
for I am both and neither
righteous and ruthless

i am fire

they all want to touch me
they all say i look hot
bright
powerful
beautiful
but don't understand
all the ways they will burn
if they come too close

only the most skilled and patient
can ignite the fire in my heart
into a steady loyal blaze
and each time i hope for someone
who knows how to gently guide
softly control
and steadily feed the fire that i am
but time and time again
they become addicted to the adrenaline
of trying to hold something so free and wild
and against warning, they get much too close
promising they're strong enough to handle me

i consume them

and while the flames of who i was
turn to soft gray dust
slipping through the fingers of insanity
my smoke darkens the sky with the regret
of every bridge i've burned
selfishly destroying everything good around me

and when i finally have nothing left
the embers in my veins
refuse to die out
as i attempt to hold on to
the death of what could've been
they all want to touch me
they say i look hot
bright
powerful
beautiful
but they don't understand
all the ways they will burn
if they come too close
and how my embers
will refuse to let go
even as I hurt them

all or nothing

i'd rather die in agony
from the
rawness of the love
i have for you
then ever be satisfied
with the apathy
of being
with anyone else

speech obstruction

what i call her is four syllables
her real name three syllables
her nickname two syllables
what i feel for her one syllable
yet it's the one
i can barely get out of my throat

i wish i was good

when manipulation
was woven into my being
from days before I knew my alphabet
how could I ever learn to love
without strings attached

softening

so when at last
the granite imbedded
into her face
softened into laughter
i knew
she was the only one
that would ever
make me believe in love

for years, i've known

i was 16 when i met you
days prior to my birthday
i was in a new place
a new state
and nothing was ok
but your deep eyes
and even deeper wisdom
melted away my shell
showing me compassion
through my confusion
i blurted out, "are you gay?!"
i just had to know
if there a sliver of a chance
the left side of your lips curled
into a smile as you shook your head in denial
but i wasn't convinced
i was convinced that
i needed to know your soul
i was 16 when i knew you were the one

i was 17 when i got to know your soul
we whispered secrets to each other
and we read the pages of our story
that remain unknown to all but a few
you were a light in my darkest times
offering a hand to pull me out of my own pit
and wrapping your arms around me
to keep me safe from myself
you were unlike anyone i'd ever known
and i dreaded the day i knew would come
the day i had to let you go
i was 17 when I knew you were the one

i was 18 when i had to let you go
I moved to a state far away
and our goodbyes cut me to my core
i knew we could never be together
so i poured out everything to a friend in georgia
and waltzed with the heart of a dancer in delaware
i jumped in the deep end with an abuser in oregon
but none were you

yet after awhile
you came back into my life
we picked up where we left off
all others fell away from my interest
i wrote you letters of my love
knowing you'd break my heart yet caring not
i was 18 when i knew you were the one

i was 19 when you broke my heart
you led me to believe i was wanted
we spent hours on the phone each day
talking late into the night till you fell asleep
we were closer than ever before
so in a decision of rash trust in you
i took a bus to the nearest airport
flew across the country
with a passion only the gays will understand
and climbed in taxi for three hours
all to come see you
it was all worth it the second
i saw that smile, those eyes
heard that voice, that laugh
felt those soft hands on my back
heard that heartbeat beneath my ear
breathed in that fragrance on your neck
tasted those lips
oh god, those lips

you held me in your arms
and you kissed me
and *you* kissed me
and you kissed *me*
and for few days, i thought
that my wildest dreams had become
my sweetest reality
that we had rearranged the constellations
to spell out our names together
that everything that had ever happened
was just a path leading to
the best thing that ever happened to me...
being with you
although i knew it wouldn't last
i couldn't see how i could ever let you go
i was 19 when you told me you loved someone else

i was 20 when i couldn't let you go
i stopped hungering for the love
you couldn't give me
but could never settle for less than you
i tried to move on to other women
and my phone was abuzz with flirty texts
but nobody could ever begin
to take your place in my heart
i won't ever chase after you again
but I'll be right here
if you ever change your mind
i was 20 when i saved a place for you

I'm 24 now
I still think of you

but you're too afraid

and from the mists
will appear a clarity of vision
one that will part the curtains
of regretted mistakes littering our past
to view an awaited future
strong and pure

and from the darkness
will appear a soft light above
whispering of things unknown to us
like hope, like love, like trust
but the light refuses to come to us
we must reach for it

and from beneath the icy chains
will appear a tender warmth
after so many years of seclusion
these feelings must be coaxed into verbal words
taking time and care
let us learn this art
of unraveling fear

may we meet again

i loved you
i love you even still
i will love you
in the next lifetime

PART 2

the ways i broke

wee hours

when it's the wee hours of morning
the ones often confused with night

the ones in which we once whispered dark secrets
to each other over the safety of a long-distance call
the ones where the moon shines the very brightest
and the stars splatter the dark sky like sparkles
the ones where you'd tell me of the song
that you heard that day
and i'd play it over and over
softly singing with a smile
playing at the side of my lips

the hours that i now dread
the ones where the lack of your voice is deafening
the ones where sleep taunts
the very edges of my soul
the ones i spend in void attempt
to discover where i went wrong
and why my arms remain empty
instead of wrapped around you

when it's the wee hours of morning
the ones often confused with night
do you ever remember all that we shared
in our ephemeral synchronization

bloom where planted

am i rooted?
or did the earth just swallow
the deepest parts of me
never to see light again

with beauty

i fell with beauty
like late fall leaves
crumbling into pieces
between the fingers of a closed fist
drifting towards the ground
fading away, dying,
but not before they shone with a magnificent palette of colors
illuminating all the cloudy streets
through the months that
only have a hint of cold
as summer drifts into our yesterdays

she
was a branch to hold onto
but harsh winds came…
she let go of me
and i just fell…

        fell…

                fell to the ground

but in a way that caught the eye
i crumbled away in a flash of color
i broke in a way that was lovely
i broke hard and i broke loud
and anyone who looked into my eyes could
see the fractures
across the surface of my heart
hear the cracking

loud and head turning
feel the breaking
awful and frightening
and yes
i wanted it known i hurt
and i hurt horribly
i wanted it known i missed her
and i missed her terribly
i wanted it known i loved her

and i loved her
oh how i loved her
i wanted it known
that yes, i fell
but i fell with beauty
for though i crumbled to bits when i hit the ground
i didn't stay down
i stitched myself back together
with glamorous thread and a gold needle
and crafted my own self
into a creation of art
i chased after the pieces of myself
that got lost somewhere in between
"i love you" and
"you mean nothing to me"
and i caught each one
putting them back into place

making myself whole once more
then i rose up
and i rose up with a force
showing all what it looks like
to fall
and to fall terribly
but to fall
with beauty

not enough metaphors

the memory of your voice
bounces around the inside of my skull
like a perpetual echo

the feel of your soft caresses
taunt me like the hope one feels
on the first day of spring

the smell of your perfume
lingers like an undesired houseguest
that has outstayed their welcome

each night i lie awake
and still i remember
every last moment i spent
in your arms
wishing only to return
to their warm safety

but i also remember the way it ended
the way I couldn't breathe after you drove away
as if you were my only oxygen
the way my trust shattered
like fine china carelessly thrown to the ground
the way the sobs rocked my body to sleep
knowing i was never going to be good enough for you

this montage of recollections replays in my head
over and over and over
twisted together
like the sweetest nightmare
that i'm bound to
without hope of ever waking from
you broke me

walking away

i had my mind set
i had my mind so set after you broke my heart
i was simply going to walk away
and not even consider
stopping to glance back in your direction
but you had other plans
and in the last of a hundred fleeting moments
you called out to me
so that i was left with no choice
other than to turn back around
and look into your eyes one last time
even though i had my mind set
to simply walk away

go to a meeting please

i never knew if the
red liquid swirling
within your wine glass
was just a light alcohol,
bitter poison,
or my cursed blood

i guess in the end
all three became the same

absence of truth

lies
    lies
        lies
i try to make sense of it all
like a puzzle missing too many pieces
i attempt at untangling the rumors
wrapped around my throat threatening to end me
i do my best to fight a tidal wave of hatred
and stop all these lies
swiftly falling out of your mouth
with poisonous passion and earnest ease
your tongue slicing me like a sharp knife
it's all lies that you speak to me
lies
    lies
        lies

up in smoke

you took everything
i had left
and then poured
alcohol on my wounds
just to make sure
i burned alive
from our sparks

but you forgot
smoke stings the eyes
chokes the throat
and darkens the sky

protect myself

push them away
letting subconscious rule
dodge the bullets
by shooting them first
take down the opponent
wrong opponent! oops?!
sleep life away some days
and others stay awake
all through the treacherous night
dare not give love a chance
for it would destroy me entirely
manipulate the adversary
before they ever realize what is happening
cut off all support
for i am all that i need
anchors lie in dust
safety nets fill with holes
trust no man and trust no woman
and survive only on the spiked adrenaline of fear
why?
because it would only take one more knife in my back
for me to fall
and never rise again

unappreciated words

and after everything
i'm left with nothing
but a shaky hands upon a broken keyboard
and a hundred fleeting moments
that i reminisce over each night
vowing to decipher the reason
why i wasn't good enough

i thought i had the written words
that could soften the most hardened heart
and set aflame the coldest soul
but you proved
that belief to be false

if you combined the pages
of all my carefully written letters to you
you'd find yourself
holding enough words to fill a novel
cover to cover
stuffed with intense love and raw determination
but in between every page
there would lurk the knowledge
that every artful adjective
every unique simile
and all the ways i found
to elusively say
i love you
meant nothing
to you

the right to anger

just below the sweet mask
lies the deepest thinker
beneath the forged stupidity
perceptivity peers
behind the bars of laughter
intense focus hides
bubbling under the compassion
hurt and a thirst for revenge lurks
waiting
watching
striking!!
you never saw it coming
because you never should have underestimated
my darkness

dear naïve 16-yr-old me

you don't see it now
but i must warn you
beware of the one
with the succubus eyes

you will chase her endlessly,
through everything, you will love her
through every storm
through every hindrance
through every midnight
but in the end,
it will matter not

she will rip you apart,
limb from limb
with glistening teeth
that she sharpened on your whispered confessions
digging into you
deeper and deeper
leaving behind scars that may never heal
she will ensnare you,
pulling you in by all your heartstrings
and spinning you round

until you find them wrapped around your throat
gasping for truth
and grasping for reality
but left for lost
run away now
you still have time
tear your eyes away from her gaze
oh you persistent imbecile
i have warned you

love,
your 21-yr-old self

veiled pens

i cry ink onto paper
because sometimes
the tears are too rough
too heavy
too painful
too messy
and only words imbedded onto paper
could ever comprehend
the pain
the love
the loss
the anger
i turn my head downwards
incarcerate my tears
and i write…
i let my hand flow to its own rhythm
a rhythm of flowing letters and heavy ink
i cry ink onto paper
because sometimes
i can't handle the tears
and only words imbedded onto paper
could ever comprehend
the volume
of this agony

you didn't just break my heart

you broke my smile
tore it off my jubilant face
and left me with nothing more
than hot tears
welling at my eyes
choking my breaths
and i don't know that i'll ever
smile the same

you broke my spirit
once described as bubbly, strong,
and wilder than a raging forest fire
i now fail to make simple conversation
and can barely hold myself together
my sanity like a bomb
ticking, ticking
threatening to detonate at any moment

you broke my confidence
and the way i used to walk
with my head high and shoulders back
is now foreign to me
i paint my face as if it's a canvas
and walk slowly
without purpose
forgetting how poised i used to be

you broke my will
i used to believe i could
do anything
be anyone
but now doubt creeps in
the hole that you left in me
and reminds
just how worthless i am

tasting moonlight

i used to wonder what moonlight tasted like
then i kissed you
and knew

moonlight tastes…
so sweet
oh so sweet
tender but
strong enough to handle me in all that i am
moonlight tastes like something rare and wholesome
leaving me needing more
of her silvery saccharinity
even as the sun starts to rise

but moonlight leaves an aftertaste
of soft regret
hazy confusion
dark pain
and the unreachable hope
of tasting moonlight
just
once
more

destroyed

it's ok
it's alright
i knew you'd hurt me
long before i ever told you which parts of me
were defenseless
i forgive you because

the moment our eyes found contact
all the way across that room of crushed hopes
when your soul recognized mine
and i instantly knew
i'd be ok with breaking for you
with bending so far backwards
that when my spine snapped
alongside my last shred of sanity
i wasn't even surprised
i just laid there
thinking how in a heartbeat
i'd do it all again
without hesitation

i still break for you

i still trip over incessant thoughts of you

i still crumble into tears at your name

i still collapse at the thought of never holding you in my arms again

i still fall for you

and those eyes across the room

i still reach for you with arms

crushed beneath the weight of the question

i ask myself each night...

"why wasn't i good enough"

unforgettable instances

i remember every moment
we spent in the presence of each other
and i feel a painful tightness
in my weary chest
it's just my body's
way of attempting to close around the chasm
that you left in my heart
when you told me that i should go

i miss you dearly
and just as nothing can erase
the twinkling sparkles from the darkness above
nothing can erase
the memories of us
that i hide away in the darkness of my heart
the veiled secret i promised to never tell...
but in the end, i will heal
softly, surely, slowly at first
climbing out of the ashes
of every love letter i set fire to
i was created from the dust of hardship
and the fabric of resilience
but you, my secret lover
you have to live with the knowledge
of how you almost broke me

stupid decisions

i bared my vulnerabilities to you
never fearing the fact
you could sharpen your weapons
on each secret
in a hundred indifferent ways
i exposed the pieces of me
i habitually shelter
within a safe shell
made of vague metaphors and a sharp tongue
but for you i did away
with shells and walls and alarms and boundaries
i threw it all away
right along with my dignity
and self-preservation
and now i only wonder
could i have been
anymore
stupid

holding on

inhale the burning fragrance…
it is my dignity
don't breathe
or it just might disappear
into ashes
drifting away
on the unsympathetic
fingers of the wind

just stop

don't do that
i hate when you do that
i hate when you do that
you walk right past me
looking through me
as if i don't exist
as if you don't see me
as if i mean nothing
i know you see me
i know you do
i know you see the tears i'm holding back
i know you the angry words i'm biting back
i know you see me
so don't you dare walk past
without a glance in my direction
you don't get to do that
i hate when you do that
when you walk right past me
like old trash on the sidewalk
as if you can't see me
i know you can
and i know you do

and so i learned french and spanish

there are 171,476 words in the english dictionary
yet there is no string of letters
that begins to describe how i miss you

maybe i am insane

i call
and i call
and i call again
they say doing the same thing
time and time again
while expecting a different result
labels one as insane

i guess i must be terribly insane
for i keep calling
listening to my phone dial your
all too familiar number
and ring for what feels like forever
hoping you'll pick up
just like you used to
and tell me everything that happened in your day
while i play sweet love songs and
hold on to every word you speak
like it's the sole thing i need
to survive

but now
i call
and i call
and i call again
but you never pick up these days
but insane people still know how to hope

magic is merely woman made

you made me feel
as though miracles
were meant to manifest
as often as the moon

and crazy coincidences
were as common
as our conversations

i thought luck
looked like you longing
for my love
late in the night

so i never aimed for the
sparkles sprinkled across the night sky
instead
i took my best shot at the silvery moon
believing the stars beneath me
would spread like a safety net
to soften my descent

and as i fell from
the altitudes of my failed plan
flailing my arms
my fears unfolded before me
and now i feel that any
belief in phenomena
is fairly foolish

how did we ever end up here

sometimes the silence is overbearing

it washes over me

it holds me

it fills me

consuming me

choking me

clawing at my insides

yet you remain so silent

ignoring my words

pretending not to see

the fissures between us

we drift apart

like lonely continents

irreversible damage

i could handle the arguments

the exchange of bitter words

followed by a parade of apologies and promises

i could accept the inevitability of the situation

that you could never reciprocate the passion

i could deal with the flaws of us both

lips kissing bottles and words tripping over lips

i could be okay with the midnight texts and 3 a.m. calls

i could grasp the meaning of the words you chose

when smashing my bruised heart

but the silence

the silence stabbing into me

is too much

this silence is a jolting thing

leaving me feebly scratching at the walls you built up

begging for answers and cursing this

fucking

silence

heights of high

i never feared limitations
until i met you
i feared the way
you'd take me to new levels
lifting me up
rising by my side
until i fell for you
and you cast me away
under the pretenses of
the impossibility of us
breaking my bones
upon impact with
the cold reality
i'll always be second place

now i'm mad

i can feel it boiling
inside my sternum
tumultuous emotion tormenting
the bones of my ribcage
scorching my inner organs
letting all your threats
towards myself and my kin
be the gasoline
setting off a fiery anger
deep inside of me
do be careful
i might just decide
to make sure
you burn too

cerulean

i won't tell you my favorite color
for with time it will become quite obvious
but i will tell of the color that i detest

gray

with her veiled answers
and shrouded despondency
gliding through the befores and afters
of every failed relationship
leaving to wonder
about every color our relationship could've been

a serene blue perhaps
or maybe a fiery orange
a voracious lipstick red
or an adventurous green
a royal and regal purple
or possibly an inspiring yellow

but now it's just gray
the color of unanswered questions
and i
hate
the color gray

blind

like a twig between your fingers
you broke your promise
to always be there
for months you fed me
these lies
these lies
these lies
and i looked into
those eyes
those eyes
those eyes
but i remained
unwise
unwise
unwise
so now you hear
my cries
my cries
my cries
i wish we could rewind every clock
and turn back every calendar
so i could leave you behind
and forget every promise
that you broke
like a twig between your fingers

now i get it

i'd so rather have

a vodka-soaked tongue
only declaring tomorrow's regrets

and a tequila-burned throat
easing the left side of my chest

and rum-flavored cheeks
filled of something that is not hope

then to ever again
taste the memory of
your lips
beneath mine

cursed night

above me
far beyond my reach
flashed a shooting star
i thought to wish upon it
but decided against the notion
due to the insensitive
riskiness of magical moments
so instead of wishing
upon the taunting star
i cursed it
i tilted my head upward and
i cursed a shooting star
I cursed it

is that my reflection?

she drifted
her voice became foreign
yet she spoke the same language as before
it was quieter yet wilder
with a hint of irrationality
it had an edge
yet still tinged with compassion

she wandered
until nothing was familiar
travelling from city to city
in desperate search for something
that could never be explained
with just words
but perhaps the tip of a paintbrush
could tell you

she strayed
soon the words she once spoke
lost their power and magnetism
and every word was no longer
clung to and adored by others
so she became silent

she needed a way out
actually
she just needed a way back

the daze of the year

you dragged my heart
across a calendar
of lustful grief-filled days
summers consisted of
empty bottles and
stumbling words
fall had me ignoring
the shift of the colors
as I pined after you
winter caught me by surprise
the morning air
competing with the coldness
beating beneath my ribcage
and spring left me with
torn up letters never sent
bloody nailbeds
and noise complaints from
the neighbors
only for summer to insist
we make another round
through the months

my pride, my murderer

try to hurt me
but like a scorpion
i will sting my own self to death
before ever being defeated
by something stronger

confused

and the worst part
is what if it was my fault
did she lure me
or did i lure her
or
even worse
did love plunge me
into the icy waters of
delusion

did she ever love me
or was it a dream

did she ever want me
or was it a wish

did she ever care for me
or was it a fantasy

skin-deep confidence

i was once asked why
i don't cover my scars
that are so plain to see
upon my arms
i made a face of confusion
and replied,
"but i do cover them"
i cover my scars with a daily hunt
for validation
from people who matter not
i cover my scars by controlling
and limiting my food intake
i cover my scars with laughter that's just a little
too loud to be natural
and brief smiles hidden behind
chewed down fingertips
because i hate my teeth but would never tell
i cover my scars by dwelling on what could've been
because i'm terrified of starting again
and would rather chase what i know is impossible
then risk being rejected by what is possible
i cover my scars by making damn sure everyone else
knows they're smart and beautiful and amazing
for i know what it's like to never hear those words

i cover my scars by doing my best
to bandage another's wounds
wiping away fresh blood and stitching them up
as if in playing savior, i might just be able to heal too
i cover my scars by walking in a way
that catches the eye
shoulders back, chin up, eyes set, back straight, brisk pace
because who knows,
if i walk too slow
my past might catch up with me
i cover my scars by creating art
in which they can all see the ways
i've squeezed every drop of beauty out of my pain
and created priceless masterpieces with it
i cover my scars by never telling where they came from
and creating elaborate stories of how i
"fell from the heights of a ladder as a child"
and tell it in a way that ensures
everyone is laughing by the end
never to realize the ugly truths in my hideous scars
but i don't even bother covering them with
makeup or long sleeves or tattoos
because what they'll never understand is
these scars go so much deeper
than just my skin

this is why

i breathe in the scent of confusion
laced with deceit
i breathe out hurt
i breathe out hate
i breathe out everything that's a mix of the two
BE SILENT!!
don't you dare speak your addictive lies to me
i see the guilt squirming in your eyes
this is why...

you come into my life muttering promises
of truth and peace
yet you leave just as fast
without a trace of evidence of your every whispered oath
BE STILL!!
don't you dare walk out of my life
leaving me to lie in the embers of our façade
this is why...

you raise your shaking fists above me
bringing them down with a force equal
to the hidden rage in my heart
i cover the bruises yet still bleed
BE GONE!!
don't you dare try to come back
after you've greedily exhausted every last chance i gave you
this is why…
this is why i trust nobody
this is why i keep my walls higher than an eagle can soar
and this is why i refuse to love

lip tattoo

i asked you
how you'd feel if i got a lip tattoo
you jokingly declared
you'd cease to talk to me

months later
our bodies laid together
the universe sewing our fate
with the shortest thread of a moment
our spirits weaved together
as if we were our own net
to save each other
you pressed your mouth to mine
and you tattooed your name
all over my lips
in the invisible ink
of promises perceived
between the blinks of your eyelids
and true to your word
you ceased to speak to me

twisted bones

i am a pile of
impulsive decisions
defense mechanisms
scribbled therapy notes
and countless things never said
topped with the crumbles of a broken heart
on the edge of a road to god knows where

but what they'll never understand is that
the guilty only
wish to redeem themselves
for things they did long ago to protect themselves
and the thief only
wishes to give back
what they never received

the hypocrite only
has lived on the other side
and is begging you
not to follow similar footsteps
and the liar only
wishes to create a better narrative
then the dark truth
and was never heard
when telling the truth of the abuse
an entire stolen childhood
was flooded with lies told
about "how terrible they were"
the manipulator only
thirsts for a drop of control
in a timeline twisted by more trauma
than any horror writer could ever imagine
and the sinner only
wishes to be the angel in someone's life
that they themselves prayed for
but never came across

i am made of these poisons
crafted into my twisted backbone
but what i am not
is a bad person
poison can still be medicine
in small amounts

in pictures

they always show lions
with their beautiful manes
sprawled across boulders
poised solemnly in tall grasses
with an essence of beauty and power

but they never show the warm blood
dripping from their faces
their paw still on the belly of their prey
breaths heavy from the chase
fur matted from the grapple
doing what they must
to survive

a beauty portrayed
but still
a beast inside

just one sign

i stood on the edge of the bridge
the water seeming to sing a death lullaby
the promise of ending this pain luring me
taunting tempting teasing
i gripped the cold steel railing with arms
that have been decorated with cuts scars and burns
i looked upward at the night sky
and promised myself through the tears
"if i can find one star in this blinding dark, i shall go on"
but i could find not one
i searched east
peered west
stared north
and gazed south
but to no avail
there was no star to pin my hope upon
not a single flickering dot appeared above me
and so i drew in a breath
preparing the last of my courage to jump
into the abyss of the hungry black water

PART 3

the ways i healed

feel the fallen façade

maybe we have to feel the wounds
to experience the healing
and connect with that which is inside each of us
hope…
raging hope seething from within, even
as we bleed
as we scream
as we cry

we must gaze into the flames
into the reflection of our souls
to evoke what we know but ignore
passion…
burning passion igniting our hearts, even
as we bleed
as we scream
as we cry

we have to whisper into night
so we may fall into peace with our own fears
and find what we chase endlessly
love…
unwavering love writhing beneath perception, even
as we bleed
as we scream
as we cry

be your own peace

if broken sticks of charcoal
can find a new purpose in the hands of an artist
why must we strive to be whole
to be perfect
why not accept our damaged loveliness
as a part of something greater

if light really does shine better
through a shattered vase
why must we struggle to cover our flaws
to hide insecurities
why not display our imperfections
as a part of something greater

if stars only do shine
in the late lunar hours
why is it that we run from the dark
from the unknown
why not embrace the blackness of the night
for without
the stars would simply blind us

the difference between attachment and connection

for my first love
i'd sacrifice myself to the cliffsides
to be like the mythical Alcestis
but for my second love
i'd be sure we were nowhere near
any dangerous cliffs
for my first love
i'd give my body to the underworld
mirroring the risks of Orpheus
but for my second love
i'd always be there for her
hanging on by a thread
just to hold her up
as if I was Atlas
and she, my whole world

and as for my third love?
i'd do anything for them...
but with boundaries
i love them without
obsession
i hold them without
uncontrollable lust
i give without
losing myself
for to love without grounding
is to cosplay as Icarus

the parts of me you buried

i stretched out my arms to the sun
searching for the old light in me
that i could never find these days
but I was only left blinded

i bowed my head in prayer
begging every religion for an answer
but the darkness around me
remained all too silent

i mirrored a wilted dandelion
losing hope with each day
wishing only for just
a little more strength

then finally i took a breath
and grounded myself
stretching my roots deep enough
to finally find the parts of me
that you buried long ago

a sunflower, not a raindrop

i thought
i was falling for you
but only because
you turned my world upside down
the truth is not that i am falling
but that i am growing

trapped waves

like a polished seashell
i held you to my ear
and let your depths
tell me the story of the ocean

leo + cancer

I am a goddess
Even though
Still enveloped
By the disaster of you

mama said say thank you

i want to thank you
thank you for the way you pulled my heart out
from its apathetic hiding place
and lit a fire in it
when times could not have gotten any darker
thank you for teaching me to fall in love

and thank you for leading me on for so long
even though it was confusing
and a long treacherous path
with me chasing you to no end and
stopping at nothing to show you love
thank you for teaching me patience

and thank you for breaking me
it hurt more than physical pain
and in enduring the aftermath
i doubted i would ever make it through
but i did
thank you for teaching me i don't need you to survive

good luck forgetting me

she tossed me out
with everything else she didn't want
she left me behind
with everyone else she didn't have time for

and as i took heavy steps away
in the opposite direction
it took everything in me not to turn around
not to stop
not to run back to her
to tell my shaking heart
that everything will be ok
and will my legs to not waver
in carrying me away with dignity
at the end of it all
the hardest thing
i ever did
was to keep walking

she thinks she's tossed me out
with everything else she didn't want
she thinks she's left me behind
with everyone else she didn't have time for
but she will soon discover
how wrong the assumption is

i am the girl
that is entirely unforgettable

my laughter invading her memories
will remind her of what she lost
my lips in the back of her mind
will evoke regret in what she did
my poise will appear in clear recollection
to make her wonder what could've been
my letters she'll find in an old drawer
and she will wish she had chosen me

she will at last realize she did not toss me away
with everything else she did not want
she will at last realize she did not leave me behind
with everyone else she had no time for
for my memory made itself a home
in the forefront of her mind

good luck forgetting
a girl
who learned long ago
how to become
entirely unforgettable

everything in my power

with stones slick from crying eyes
with the ground indented from stomping feet
with air scratched by desperate hands
with bottles empty from a search for tranquility
with walls echoing the screams of fear
with hands scarred by my own loyalty
i tried to create a world
in which we could be together
only to watch every desperate effort
crumble away into memories
and finally
i can say
that it's okay

because the love is dead

sometimes
the memory
needs a funeral
and the love letters
demand a cremation
and the longing that lingers
requires a gravestone

played

do i look like a tic-tac-toe game?
something to be played?
someone to be manipulated?
is that the perception
that you have of me?
do i seem like the type of girl
that will bow to your every demand
like a peasant without dignity
that i will be your loyal bitch
to fill in all the holes she left in you
that i will bend over backwards
until i snap in two
is that the perception
you have of me
do i appear brainless
someone clueless to your plot twists
and oblivious to your elaborate schemes
is that the perception you have of me
cuz if it is,

oh darling
you need to get those eyes checked

thorns and scars

in the end of all things tragic
the greater courage will always
lie in the heart of the one
that lets go
rather than the one who
holds onto the wicked thorns
of a once beautiful rose
even as their fingers stain red
from a bleeding past
ignoring the sight of
petals curling and falling away
descending to the cold ground below

be brave
open your shaking curled fingers
and let go
let those falling petals carry away
every self-doubt
every midnight fear
every unanswered query
every lingering regret

the once beautiful rose

can no longer bring beauty

into your life

its over

and there is no reason

to continue bleeding from open scars

wounds inflicted by the thorns of what was

let go

just let go

let go

let it all out

and for a moment
my anger felt
like a pair of wings
lifting me out of my pit
i unleashed pure fury braided with hurt
i inquired about all
the things i wondered of at night
i let go of the hesitation in my voice
and did away with empathy
i yelled
i screamed
i cried
i broke
i questioned
i broke
i drank
I broke
I drank
I broke
I drank
I arose
i survived
i breathed
i forgave

and then it was over
i was free from my own emotions
the chains fell away from
the bars upon my lips
my heart became free once more

ready for someone new at last

i don't need your advice

hush!
be with me
as the depths of the winding river
teach me how to still the raging waters
in my own skull
hush!
watch with me
as the emerald fields of grass sway
beneath a stormy sky
and the winds force me to my knees
hush!
study with me
the habits of sweet little birds
as they cheerily hop along
blind to my dark anxiety
hush!
listen with me
to the voices of angels
carried on wisps of wind
sending me on my way
do not dare speak aloud
and shatter the fragility of this moment
this is me healing
hush!
this is me healing

nursed by nature

i always welcome the stormy skies
for they never fear me
each drop caressing my face
with tender force
coating my tongue in purity
and brushing away my tears
never asking answerless questions
like "are you ok?"
the tender droplets already know i'm not
and so they crash down to the earth
right beside my hopeless form
and reminds me in a whisper
"my darling
falling can be lovely"

reasons to travel

the ebb and flow of the inevitable
the constancy of things not constant
the consistency of people not consistent
the familiarity of places not familiar
it is all i've ever known

wild and unfree

there were no limitations
in her mind
yet she could never quite grasp peace

the wind and sky were free and called her name
begging to claim a piece of her wild spirit
but never could she fully give herself to the wind

because the earth and nature in its divine elegance
also pleaded for the rare depths within her

neither the wind and sky
nor the earth and nature
could keep her
so she broke herself in two
to please them both
and anger neither
she gave her mind to the wind and sky
and her body to the earth and nature

the broken girl then carried on
floating in a space known to few
known only
to those named
poets

after the blood is washed away

the thing about
being hurt
is scar tissue
is so much tougher
than unmarred skin

i dare you to lie

look me in my glinting eyes
then tell me i'm not strong enough
touch my red waves of hair
then tell me i'm not soft enough
press my scarred body against your unblemished one
then tell me i'm not poised enough
hear the screams from my nightmares
then tell me i'm not innocent enough
rip my tongue out with your teeth
then tell me i'm not sweet enough

go on,
poison this air with these lies
tell me i'm not enough
tell me
i
am
not
enough
i dare you

beneath a shooting star

and in that moment
i knew
i would never quite
be the same girl
but yet
it bothered me none
i learned from what
you put me through

symptoms of a warrior

once i put down the blade
i thought it was buried
once my wounds had healed
i thought the fight was over
so unexpected was the
bleeding ghost of my youth
coming back to life
placing that razor back in my hand
visions of old habits invading my brain
convincing me to make just one more cut, just one

once i put down the calorie sheet
i thought it was buried
once i learned how to eat again
i thought the fight was over
until one day an apple looked disgusting
shadows seemed to laugh at me in disgust
and my mouth turned away from food again

once i put down the bottle
i thought it was buried
once i learned to turn down party invites
i thought the fight was over
until a friend gifted me the liquid of tomorrow's regret
and left after i passed out in the living room
spinning in circles of the past

once i put down the toxic relationship
i thought it was buried
once i blocked that number
i thought the fight was over
until they messaged me with trick apologies
promising they just wanted to be friends
sucking me into the enabling game

once i put down the past
i thought it was buried
once i moved on towards healing
i thought the fight was over
what i didn't know
is that it's never over
each morning when my toes brush the carpet
i choose to fall back into the ways of yesteryears
or continue to become who i want to become

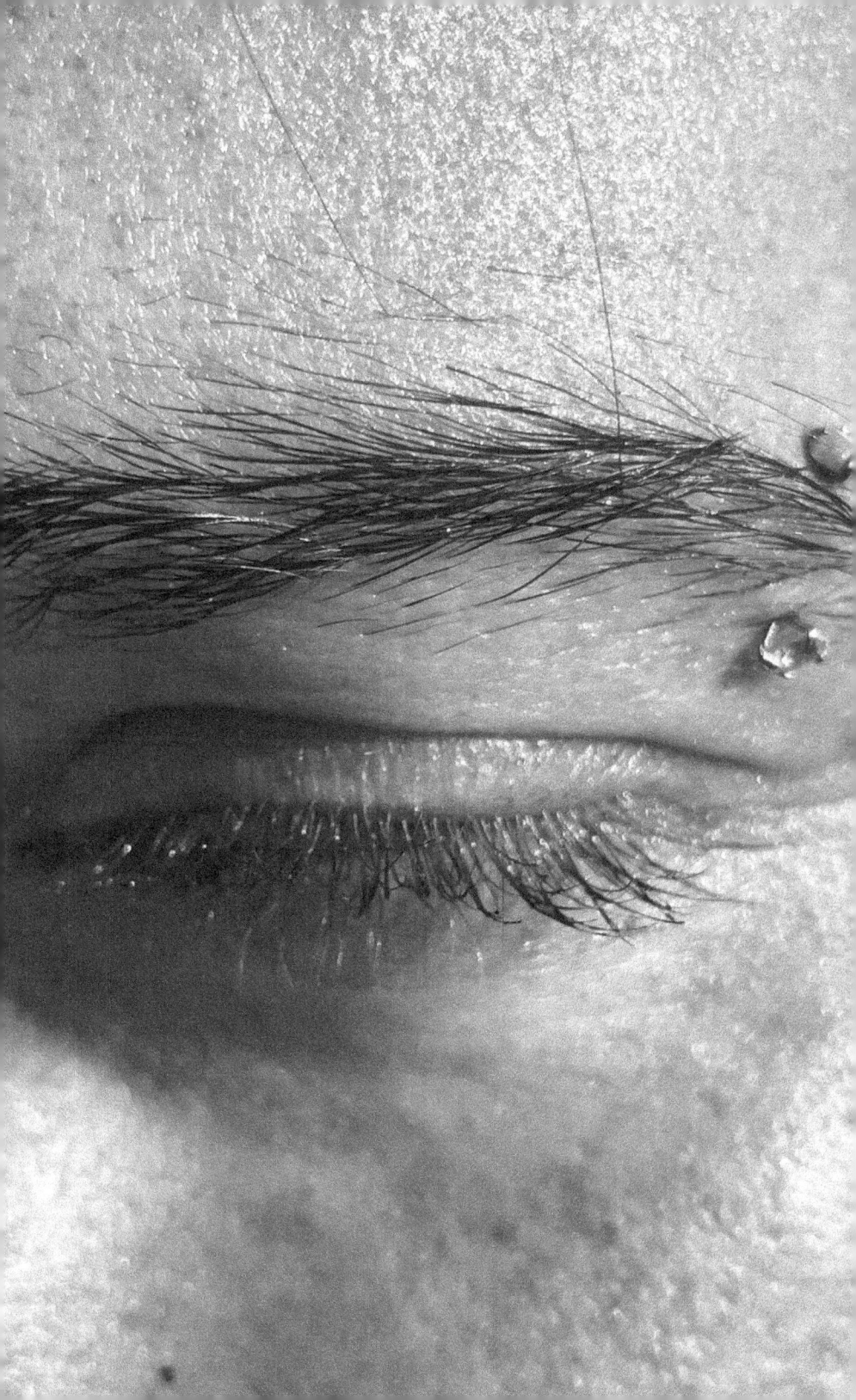

you have no idea how strong i am

she said i wasn't strong enough to hold her
baby i'm plenty strong enough
but i carried everyone else for so long
now it's time for me to carry myself

but, darling, lean on me
and we'll be on our way

history

"but you were my girl," cried the miserable one

"and now i'm a force to be reckoned with," replied the healed one

tempest

a wound always takes longer to be healed
than to be inflicted
i must be wary
of using my own
razor-sharp tongue
to lick my wounds

addiction

if i don't long for a bullet
lodged inside my bones
and i do not long for a blade
opening my throat
and I do not long for a hammer
pounded into my skull
why then do i long for a woman
to torture my soul

the past no one knows about

i looked evil in the eye
yet somehow
clutched to the last of my innocence
i never experienced being a child
and have lost more people than can be counted
i carved my own skin with razors
in an outnumbered battle with my own brain
i stomped on every looming statistic
and fought against odds stacked higher than everest
i loved with all my strength
and chased loyalty like it was
the last morsel of oxygen on the planet
and after all that
you'd think i'd be weakened
or quietly beat down
but not i

i learned how to stack the bricks thrown at me
and built a stairway to a better life
i bare every scar as a reminder
of the days that sculpted me into who i've become
i threw the noose up into the sky
and used it to climb towards my dreams
i set fire to every barrier
smiling through the smoke
and like an injured phoenix
with shaky confidence
i reclaimed my life so that
nothing
can
destroy
me
now

to her future lover

i'm letting her go
but promise me
promise me you'll love her with depth
and stand by her with loyalty
remind her that its ok to cry
but hold her hand when she does
be the reason she smiles and laughs
and never betray her trust
make time for her despite a busy schedule
surprise her with little gifts
never leave her wondering where she stands with you
for too many have done so to her before
listen to her words but listen closer to her silence
it speaks volumes
if you fight, watch your tongue
words said in a second can hurt for a lifetime
and never hold things against her
take her to dinner take her to that movie she's been wanting to see
take her on a road trip take her on a picnic, take her on a cruise
take her to the beach, take her to another country
take her from me but take her everywhere
remind her she's stunning each morning
and hold her through the long nights
be patient with her through it all

as everything she does has a backstory to it
be a rock for her when nothing else is solid
take care of her,
as you would the rarest flower in the world
i'm letting her go
but promise me
promise me you'll love her with depth
and stand by her with loyalty

to withstand the storms

those of us who are
rooted and grounded
have seen
the darkest parts
of the earth

no longer

i no longer need you
to function
i no longer must call
when the slightest thing
goes wrong
i no longer go sleepless
on the nights i don't
hear your voice
but
i miss you
and i want you
no less than i did before
i need you no more
but i'll want you forever

shifting perspective

one day i woke up
and with acceptance
i realized
I would never again
lay my eyes
upon your beauty
nor did i ever
wish to

cheers to missing you

rum could never taste
as sweet as her lips
tequila could never flow
as smooth as her words
cognac could never look
darker than her eyes
and the clink of a thousand glasses
could never
sound like her laughter
and so i pushed the drinks away
and grounded myself
in the truth
we will never
be together

and that's okay

full circle trap

i used to have so much love for myself
i squeezed myself out from the clutches of depression
self-talked my way out of anorexia
coped through every ptsd episode
to become a beautifully confident and bold woman
i used to be in love with who i had become

until i saw everyone else...

with their beautiful faces marred with sadness
shoulders drooping from regret
walking around with self-esteem lower than
their posture
and i wondered what i could do

i wiped away their sadness with
my hard-earned success
i lifted them up onto
my own shoulders covered in healed scars
i eased their pain with
all that i had chased after for myself
i gave all those who didn't know their worth
a piece of my own pride

until i had none left
and all those who i stood by with loyalty
had gone away on their new paths
leaving me in the exact place
i had once escaped from
leaving me in the exact place
i had once helped them escape from

titles

please don't go
don't leave me unwritten
never to return
so many things unsaid

too many almosts
surrendering to gravity
surrendering into the ashes

S.E.E.
the moonlight above
a paper storm
turn the page
its better left unsaid

dancing in the dark
craters
with a monster
inside my head

ace of hearts
checkmate

you could have stopped the pain

you knew
i would throw myself
upon the rocky shores
of your love
if given the smallest chance

and you let me

you lured me in
knowing what lay ahead
you let me tear my skin
and break my bones
and bash my head
upon the boulders
of your indifference

i survived
but barely

you did not break me
but you did not save me either
and i don't know what's worse

paralyzed hand of a writer

and for awhile
i stopped writing
i was afraid
to give you any acknowledgment
any power
lest you slither your way back into
the forefront of my mind
halting my healing process
and seizing the sanity
i worked so hard to regain

but the truth is i was not yet healing
i was still in the clutches of torment
and the throes of distress

now as i sit here
returned to my desk
to write of
the ways i healed from you,
i realize how many times
i thought i was here
healing is never linear
there are good days
and then there's the days i think of you
i will never forget you
but i do forgive you
and that
is healing

rupi kaur days…

i read the saddest of poetry
the ones tucked in the pages
i used to drown myself in
hanging on to each line like only it could hear me
rereading each word as if that would cure me
flipping the pages in a maniacal attempt to feel better
yet i no longer attach myself
when i read books of pain and grief
have i healed
or become numb

please mr. sandman

i still go to see her,
the woman i loved
she still comes to see me,
the one she left behind

but it is with closed eyes
and beneath a glittery sky
tucked into the warmth
she never gave me
i still go to see her
and she still comes to see me
but only in my dreams

the end of the world

i used to lie hopelessly
on a cold floor
hoping
for the end of the world

i'd envision the relief
in a blink
of a nuclear blast
in a second
of a tsunami
in a moment
of an asteroid
far too quick
for any comprehension

so i could just float away
faultlessly
into nothing
and they would all blame
the end of the world

but then
i began a journey
a journey to joy

i went everywhere
and anywhere that felt safe
i did everything
i ever wildly dreamed of
i challenged every thought

with defiant grace
and devoured every obstacle
with teeth sharpened on desperation
i thrust my hands into walls
and commanded them to crumble
i dragged myself inch by inch
and demanded a better life for myself
a life of joy

and i found
i think i found
it
i think i finally found joy
twisted around old thoughts
and wired with anxiety
fueled by a need for something more
i found myself
i am joy

now it matters not
if the world ends
and i do not fear it
but i long ago
stopped hoping for it
because if the world ends
it must be for a new beginning

message to the moon

i have no more messages for you
i remember a time when i did
i'd fall at the feet of your silvery glow
and beg your seeming magical essence to help me
i truly believed you held the answers
far away from me yet so seemingly in reach
i hoped for the smallest yet biggest things
a dash of luck
against odds far bigger than i
a sliver of hope
in the dead of yet another frigid night
a piece of sanity
to pause my reality if only for a second
i tore myself to pieces
while you went through opinions of me
as often as i adapted to new zip codes
they glorify you
the moon
idly swinging through the night sky
but how could i ever wish you well
you left me lonely and hopeless
when it was Jupiter who distracted my gaze
long enough to pull me out of the hypnosis

and Venus who wiped away all of my tears
with her feminine strangeness
and the shooting stars who lifted my face
it was the milky way who made me believe in miracles
and the sun who warmed me and told me i was of her
you are but a lost asteroid caught
in the orbit of this
dying planet
and i am kira nicole mikaylah aphrodite millar johnson
i have no messages for you

you knew better

perhaps it wasn't all your fault
maybe it was mine

you were a fucking grown adult
i was a weak-kneed, barely legal teen
you should have either
loved me with all you had
or immediately cut it off
instead of luring me in
knowing you
should never
and would never
and could never
love me

but perhaps it wasn't all your fault
perhaps i dragged you
into dragging me

no
it was your fault

I'm Not Over It

i have a confession i must make
a lie to be brought to plausibility
i have spread round this false claim
proclaiming it to be the truest thing
and yet when i do,
my bottom lip twitches
and my gaze shifts left to right to up to down
so i confess to you...
i...
no
    no
        no
i take it back
there's nothing to confess
i'm definitely over her
(*bottom lip twitches*)

the sound of before

i heard your voice again
many years later
it was the same warm husky low voice
that i had damn near lost myself in
you said i sounded happy
i suppose i was
but not till many years later
you just left a crater in my life
and i just chose to plant daffodils there
and water them with my tears
promising myself to arise
as soon as they had taken to blooming
when they would lift their face
as would i
but i didn't know it would be many years
before they had even begun to sprout

atomic origins

And I know
It to be true
That my atoms were formed
In the belly of a star
Because I still burn

wrioter

you really thought
i'd let it go
let you live
with the damage
you inflicted upon me
oh no
i've simply been
nursing my wounds
lying in wait
like a snake in tall grasses
for the perfect moment in time
to expose you
for the terrible human you are
you ruined me
you ruined me on purpose
forever
now you will feel
what i felt
forever

the things i did to get here

i shall soak my scars
in the saltwater of the sea
so i may leave
these blood-streaked sins
at the ocean's darkest depths
drowning myself in the waves
until my self-hatred suffocates
and i am
washed clean
whole

last chance

i despise the phrase last chance
for what even is a last chance?
the final wisp of a lit flame?
the premonition of an ending?
the fear of a lingering regret?
or could it be
the potential of a new chance?
is a last chance simply the last emotion
before stepping into a new era of self
one in which the previous reality
and all of its warring thoughts is left behind
and the new reality
is met with a receptive mind
and open spirit
i believe we have the ability to bend ourselves
around every painful ending
and let it go
with resilience and tenacity
courage and awareness
we need not call it a last chance
when it could simply be a doorway to a
new path

golden paradox

I was born in the fire
A leo from first breath
A lioness prowling this new world
A gold dripping rarity born into chaos
Capable of destruction and malice
Yet wielding grace in the form of mercy
Giving definition to the word soft

i loved again

Laying on their chest
That summer night
I felt another's warmth
As if for the first time
They were
Soft
As a whispered lyric
Tender
As a tulip unfolding itself
Raw
As a photograph underwater
Sweet
As a taste of outside this galaxy
Gentle
As a moon above raging seas
And I am
Sour impatient aggressive broken rage
But that one summer night
Laying on their chest
I found I was still capable of love

the veil of night

do not speak to me of your fears
when it was always the night that loved you

while the inescapable day held a
feeling of purposelessness
and pounding fear
of anything other than
staying in bed
lest the sun in the sky burn your irises

but the ever-loyal night invited you to
never miss a chance to dance
moving your feet beneath
the astrological disco in the sky
with the drunken flavor of life itself
lingering on two pairs of lips

the inescapable day demanded
you drag yourself up at a proper hour
submit to your life draining 9–5
slap on a halfway convincing smile
as you gaze upon your mountain range
of duties and responsibilities
and face your anxieties, horrors and guilts
under the blaze of the sun for all to see
but the ever-loyal night,
she protected you
she shielded the sight of your tears
with a cloak of darkness

and promised not to tell
secrets whispered below
the safety of nighttime

the night loved you
the day never did
so how dare you glorify the light of day
and so quickly fear the dark of night

www.ingramcontent.com/pod-product-compliance
Lightning Source LLC
LaVergne TN
LVHW091252080426
835510LV00007B/222